Nature

Nature Without

N J King

BookLeaf
Publishing

Presentation by *BookLeaf Publishing*

Web: www.bookleafpub.com

E-mail: info@bookleafpub.com

ISBN: 9789357441896

First edition 2023

DEDICATION

To Anthony, my husband, who encouraged me to pick up the pen again and gave inspiration for some of these poems.

Also Kerra and Ruffus who kept me company, occasionally insisting on being my desk.

PREFACE

I am fascinated by the seasons. When it's summer I never want the warmth to go, but by the end of August I am looking forward to cosy jumpers, hot soup and walking over crunchy leaves. I find that feeling in February, when the earth begins stirring beneath our feet so invigorating. I wanted to put some of those feelings into words.

The poems in this collection relate to nature without (the seasons, the moon) and nature within (emotions, anxieties, relationships) and at times a blend of the two. To me these subjects are not isolated; I have found that taking the time to connect with nature and being aware of its consistent rhythms has a positive effect on my mood. I have experienced and witnessed mental ill health, such as depression and anxiety in many different forms and have found it a relief to come across the words of another which seems to be speaking my own experience, as though someone sees me.

In order for us to have good mental health we need to have a relationship with nature, and in order for the nature around us to remain healthy it needs us to engage with it and learn from it. Over these pages we'll pass through a year together, exploring Nature Without and Nature Within.

Queen of All Seasons

Snowdrop, the first most hopeful sign
Stands tall and slender, head inclined
Earth surrounds in quiet slumber
Energy pulsing, still encumbered

An eye does twitch, a gentle yawn
From 'tween soft shapely lips is drawn
As supple fingers dig the soil
A myriad of life uncoils

Stretching, sighing, creepers vying
Her every motion vivifying
Sleepily she starts to wend
To barren trees she fondly tends

Each step issues vibrant rebirth
Upon the eager fertile earth
Blossom, daffodil, jewelled crocus
Her summoning of them woke us

Blinking, dazed, we run to meet her
Our youthful, jolly, spry Demeter
Resonating latent power
As around her swells a luscious bower

As vernal gives way to verdant
She remains our tireless servant
To us she grants the fairest prize
Of lazing beneath azure skies

The days grow long as she matures
Tempting us out with its allures
Lemonade, sunshine and fresh fruits
Aquaholics clad in swimsuits

To us warm days seem without end
For us her pow'r she did expend
The crop is done, the fruit is grown
She did it all without a moan

Her peak is passed, now is twilight
Her back in bowed, hair grey and white
The jewel-like colours of the Sun
Scatter the ground, her spells undone

Still she holds the power of nature
Dare not underestimate her
Days more glor'ous than in her youth
And late year blooms do show the truth

At every single misty dawn
We wonder if she will be gone
Short'ning days, her energies wane
Until at last she leaves this plane

Left all alone, we hide inside
And warmly watch the snowflakes glide
With tales to hear and logs to burn
And evergreens boding her return

Hiemal Hymn

All is still, all is quiet
Not another soul to meet
Senses muted in the crisp air
The only sound your crumping feet

Features pale but cheeks aglow
Your mufflements pulled in tight
A merry smile bedecks your face
Though puckish winds do nip and bite

The sight of the evergreen
In its viridian vest
No longer hid by oak and ash
Makes your heart sing within your breast

White tufts dancing on the air
Cov'ring the ground in glist'ning gauze
Nature's peacemaker - snow's soft quilt
Has the po'er to enforce a pause

Now reflect and think and feel
Now it's time to charge and mend
Enjoy the produce of your toil
For soon the time to rest will end

Turning back at last to home
'fore you've gone too far astray
Where the crackling of a fire
Merrily keeps the chill at bay

You sit beside a candle
And watch daylight grow dim
Until the whole world seems to shrink
To just the room that you are in

My Greatest Fear

Some fear spiders
Or slithering snakes
Being up high
Or making mistakes
But what I've found
As I go through life
There's something deeper
That gives me my strife

The thing I fear
Is that I will find
When my time's up
And I must resign
That nothing I've done
Nothing of note
That all will be it
Away I will float

Leaving a mark
Is a natural aim
I'm sure many
Also feel the same
But it's a feeling
That can corrode
Until your whole self
Is bent on this road

I have no map
I don't know the route
Nor what's the goal
Of this vain pursuit
I just feel strongly
That surely I
Have something to give
Before I must die

Maybe it's vain
Me thinking this way
Just be yourself
I hear them all say
I try to let go
Try to be content
But it is a drive
That just won't relent

It is a fear
That can be a lure
Used by those whose
Intent is impure
So if you also
Have felt such a pain
Make sure you know
The flaws of your brain

I should have spent
In greater measures
Time learning worth
In simpler pleasures
Time being mindful
Time on gratitude
I'd have been happier
With that attitude

But then I think
If I start anew
Maybe my wait
Was finally through
So I hold on
To this crazy fear
That none will recall
I was ever here

Clumsy Little Oaf

Before we begin there's something you should know
Something I must say before I'm laid low
If you think that you've lost me and you're looking around
You'll most probably find me somewhere on the ground
I do much more falling than the leaves from a tree
I am a clumsy little oaf you see

I've glued my hands together more than once
And many a lamppost has met my bonce
I walk straight into things that have always been there
And manage to sit down on that one broken chair
Ended a meeting wearing a whole cup of tea
I am a clumsy little oaf you see

I try to help my discoordination
Restrain from undue gesticulation
I double tie laces, hold scissors point end down
Use a cable tidy, avoid overlong gowns
I get my eight hours and take Vitamin B
But a clumsy little oaf I'll always be

A Poem in Purple

The swish of the emperor's dress
Explicit sign of his noblesse
Luxury, decadence
Symbol of precedence
Of all colours sure to impress

The western tint of piety
Not just for high society
A bishop that's Lenting
Or grief now relenting
Adds to this hue's variety

The accomplishment of the sage
Pulsing core of the potent mage
Creativity flows
And experience grows
But bad luck to those on the stage

Seen in florals like glove of fox
Lavender, lupin and the phlox
A rare thing in nature
So it's valued the greater
Like crushed snails and amethyst rocks

The '60s psychedelic haze
Seen on women's suffrage displays
All shades of a bruise
As you watch it diffuse
But beware unseen UV rays

They say nothing with it can rhyme
But hirple and curple do fine
It may be a figment
But I say a pigment
Is impossible to define

Primaveral

Hard frost retreats. Sposh remains,
as earth breaks off deep winter's chains.
Bleary Sun. Fragrant rains.
Length'ning days, though night still reigns.

Below the hush, beneath the crust,
life's no longer tightly trussed.
Badger cubs grow robust.
Bulbs prepare, a final thrust.

In early morning's pale ray
roe deer stands, still clad in grey
to hear mistle thrush call from afar
wishing brumal breezes au revoir.

With the bird's farewell spoken,
dark's frosty spells are now broken.
Elder's leaf and squirrel's birth
proclaim the dawn of springtide mirth.

Returning of migratory birds;
bold chiffchaff sings uplifting words
as butterflies flit and dance,
woken from their sleepy trance

They find wildflowers now abound
across the march hares' battleground,
daffs and violets add their bloom
to decorate old winter's tomb.

Caught up in life's stress and strains,
struggles of light and dark domains,
the sense of life catching aflame
are missed
when only viewed through windowpanes.

When You Know You Just Know

How will I know it's really love?
The kind in all the books
I used to ask as a young girl
And get sympathetic looks

But really I wanted to know
And it could make me low
Though all the answer I would get
Was when you know you just know

Now that I have learnt for myself
And will soon tie the knot
I hoped to help kids just like me
But I still know diddly-squat

Nevertheless I'll do my best
To share out what I've learnt
In the hope that in your love life
You'll not get your hearts burnt

Find you someone who will laugh with you
Teach you to take a joke
But never making fun of you
Or making you feel broke

Someone who is willing to learn
The language of your heart
Can make you feel rather sublime
So make sure you do your part

If they don't like you saying no
Or respect boundaries
That should produce a big red flag
And give you much unease

And if you find you're best alone
Don't ever think that's wrong
To love yourself is a great skill
And makes your spirit strong

But if you're destined to be paired
I'll give you this advice
Take time to learn who you are first
And what are your dislikes

The big things are so important
But so the small are too
Like knowing your favourite chocolate
And how you like your brew

The one you love will enjoy you
When you're snuggled up tight
Talking, thinking, cuddling, stinking
Or when you need a respite

They'll talk with you for hours on end
When camping in a field
And they'll stay with you even when
Your darkness is revealed

It will not always be easy
To share in someone's life
It will take your dedication
To be husband or wife

So in the end how did I know
When he was on one knee
Did I wonder if this was right?
Was he the one for me?

I knew myself and he so well
I felt no fretful dread
I have to say I was so sure
It did not enter my head

Not My Cup Of Tea

'Could I just have a cup of tea?'
Is a phrase I hate to hear
It gives me chills I guarantee
And makes me come over all queer
For it is not hyperbole
To say my dear I fear
To make a cup of tea
I'll need to study for a year

'Milk and sugar?' is all I ask
I thought the job was that plain
But now it seems it's quite the task
And my head is starting to pain
I fear I have left you quite parched
Will you think I'm insane
If it's served in a flask
Or with tea leaves you have to strain?

Now do you want a builder's brew
Or milky as a pearl?
So strong it leaves a residue
Or does strong char make you hurl?
Could you please just give me a clue
If I serve up Grey Earl
Will you then start to spew
Or will your lips begin to curl?

Now do you put the milk in first
Or start off with the tea bag?
How I now with I had rehearsed
I might have avoided this agg
I find I have been so immersed
I am starting to flag
Limescale flakes have dispersed
And the guests are starting to nag

I'll pretend my kettle's broken
If you ask me for a tea
You may find you're heartbroken
If you're wanting a Rosie Lee
But if you are not outspoken
Or I find it's just me
The kettle'll be woken
And I'll enjoy my nice gnat's pee

The Mermaid's Misery - from Daughters of the Jade Isle

He was a man of mortal blood
A man of earth, fire and flood
She was a creature of the night
Magic myst'ry and moonlight

Betwixt them ran the deepest love
The kind the balladeers sing of
But secrets amidst them took growth
She held him to a solemn oath

'Come spring, come summer love will rule
I am yours through the dark to Yule
But leave me when the full moon reigns
Or never shall we be again'

Moon wax, moon wane their love remained
And at full moon her man abstained
They thought their love would ne'er abate
But they strode to a crueller fate

As month on month she took her leave
And left her absence to be grieved
Curiosity took hold
And her love he grew more bold

As the moon came to its peak
Her lover coming forth to seek
Not fearing other world magic
Saw her nature was pelagic

Seeing her in fish regalia
From lover he did turn to hater
No longer the devoted knight
His eyes he gouged at the foul sight

The lady long time did she weep
Foregoing food and drink and sleep
At that pool she did remain
Awaiting her love to come again

Come back he did in deep remorse
Drawn back by love's relentless force
For his love in vain he did seek
Though with no eyes through which to peek

She watched and wondered at his quest
That she was his goal she ne'er guessed
For fearing his detestation
She made him no communication

So they remained: she deep in grief
Him daily searching his heart's thief
Though know it not on the full moon
He'd hear her sing a woeful tune

'Though life has kept us far apart
There never were two close of heart
A love truly mine lost to trust'
Sang Morphina of Actiphus

Time For Doing

When asked my favourite season
I struggle much to answer
I think first of pretty springtime
Golden autumn and brisk winter

I never start with summer
I dismiss her out of hand
Like a beautiful lady whose
Features are commonplace and bland

Yet I find that every year
I am in for a surprise
When spring passes on her mantle
And so returns flawless blue skies

Yes the warmth upon my skin
Is a pleasurable feeling
But it's nothing so tangible
That I find to be appealing

Summer is activity
That's why it's the main event
It is outdoor socialising
It is a time being well spent

Summer is an energy
Driving impetus for fun
Playing sports day in the garden
Splashing about beneath the Sun

The calendar is teeming
Barbecues picnics and fetes
Long walks along the shoreline
Impromptu evenings with your mates

But when her golden hue has
Been entrusted to the leaves
I still don't list her virtues high
Once the fond memory recedes

One thing alone I'll recall
When frost's grasp is extending
Those long warm aestival evenings
When time felt never-ending

Give Me A Mountain

I've seen so many quotes
Provided to inspire
They talk of mountains to be climbed
To reach what you aspire

What if there is no mountain
Within the periphery
Just open plains and prairie lands
As far as the eye can see

The destination always
Stands somewhere beyond my view
I have to guess what it might be
And which path will lead me through

Just give me a mountain
I'll scale it's edge yard by yard
At least I'd know which way to go
Even if the way is hard

A wanderer passes near
Lifts me that bit higher
Their path clearly winds on ahead
But mine's just grass and briar

Choice can be a privilege
But so the morals all tell
Moderation in everything
If you want all to be well

Of course I'll take a step
Path earthy or grassed over
And pray that when the Sun hangs low
I don't wish I could change over

Entranced

There are few things that I
Find as captivating
A show this unvaried
I'd give a low rating
But every slight movement
Keeps me speculating
Each muffled utterance
Has me translating

Though at times it looks like
There's demons' eyes peeping
And my spouse up in bed
Prob'ly thinks that I'm cheating
Though the gust it produced
Has now started seeping
I just can't look away
When my dog is there sleeping

The Fall Ball

'It's time!' Ash cries, still dressed in green
descending to the floor
While lush Aspen, Autumn's golden queen
Holds back for her paramour
Blushing Maple can't believe his luck
As they join the swirling mirth
Sycamore cuts a path
With his waltz
And conker's given a wide berth

Swallows line up to watch them meet
The Sun even glances in
Autumn rain provides a steady beat
And Stag's horn blows through the din
The North Wind provides the melody
Spider a glistening shawl
The berries and Ivy
The decor
To beautify the Autumn ball

Finding My Place

'I'm stupid' I told myself when I was five,
And my smarter friends would gently deride,
My intelligence just was not that innate,
On answers I had to long contemplate.
I had to learn before I could guess,
Watching as others quickly progressed,
I tried not to let my feelings show,
But gradually I feared I was a bit slow.

I tried both my hands with the intellectuals
But I found it to be ineffectual
The academics were like a different breed,
In their world I struggled much to succeed.
Each step of theirs taking three of mine,
Like I was on a steeper incline,
I hurried away when first I could,
Desirous of somewhere where I could do good.

The intellectuals are, they often say,
Lacking common sense, so I found my way
To people with street-smarts, the savvy, the shrewd,
But their practical minds left me subdued.
Sensible, logical as they were,
Solving problems when still amateur,
Cries of 'Hold up' filled me with chagrin,
'Best leave it with us' they'd say as they cut in.

With the quick-witted thinkers I faired much worse,
Try as I might I just couldn't coerce
My brain cells to keep up with their rapid pace,
Searching for a jest to help me save face.
The speed of their minds was impressive,
But to me it all was regressive,
As I am rather introverted
Thinking on my feet left me disconcerted.

In all these years trying to keep apace
Something had formed in my cranial airspace;
From my time learning I had grown knowledge,
Something which takes years I must acknowledge.
It's then you find what wisdom you own,
From experience this skill is honed,
It's now my guide when rolling the dice
In making choices and giving advice.

At last I do know where I am fitted,
That I am no dunce, I am not half-witted.
I should feel happy, but I find inside
I'm still the five year old empty of pride.
But though this weighs so much on my mind,
Others to me are not so defined;
The size of their brain is quite apart,
What I care for is the depth of their heart.

Grandma Selene

I feel your eye as I walk up the lane
The silvery glow says you're with me again
Turning around I gaze in your face
To offer up my silent embrace

You voice no words yet somehow I hear it
As though you're speaking direct to my spirit
And whether I'm mother, maid or crone
You draw out the youth that I thought had flown

Like all grandmothers to us you appear
Kindly and slow, a gentle benign old dear
It's easy to forget just how much
Life you have known before our souls touched

Closing my eyes to end the reverie
And with a soft smile, I kiss my hand to thee
Feeling both calm and somehow revived
Sensing your presence with each lightened stride

Inkdust's Poem

You hide me in shadows
Or by key and lock
Yet still I sing out
And you I still mock

You beat me and flog me
Until I relent
Yet here I still stand
My resolve is unbent

To silence my voice
You bruise and you burn
You think you can hush me
But when will you learn

My heart is still beating
My courage is true
I will not stop writing
'til I have defeated you

Lost in Literacy

Sighing, slipping into a chair
Hot cocoa at the ready
Prepared to be taken elsewhere
A sense of thrill building already

Running her thumb along the leaves
Spine creaking as it's woken
From the tome the cover she cleaves
Like an old gate being swung open

Gingerly but eagerly she
Begins to take her paces
With a kindred spirit that be
Born of words, dialogue and phrases

Now she assumes the hero's role
Finding out that she is brave
Or seeking out a partner soul
Feeling the affection she does crave

Walking within another's shoes
And sharing in all their tears
Feeling their hopes, learning their views
All that time forgetting her own fears

Somehow it feels less daunting
To face quests in foreign lands
When the life that you're flaunting
Is secured in the writer's hands

The cocoa has gotten cold and
Beneath the throw she's curled
Her mind still in a distant land
Far from her turmoils in this world

The room has grown dark around her
She thinks, raising up her head
Is this place, now unfamiliar
Not the fictional world instead?

The Long Awaited Visitor

To some I am welcome
A retreat from what's worse
To others the end
The darkness, the curse

Some spend their whole lives in hiding from me
Some openly fight what they know has to be
But what I always say as I lift up my hood
'I've come for you friend, as you knew that I
would'

Brutal Beauty

Ethereal beauty beyond compare
His dazzling frosted white cloak
His raiment fair and his crystalline hair
Cleanse the earth in one simple stroke

Fern frost and sparkles he paints on his way
These are his glittering pride
A Yuletide display made to hide the decay
All designed to lure you outside

All changed in a sudden flurry
Your fearful heart's in a hurry
The fiend is heard before he's spied
Though shapes appear where snowflakes glide

His howl calls to you through the storm
Drowning noise of any form
As howl on howl around you rolls
Like the wails of a thousand lost souls

When it's over it's just as you feared
You've been left far from your track
Though the storm may have cleared, your
footprints disappeared
And you don't know the way to get back

This seems an endless sunrise
The sky painted a soft pink
But no warm golden prize is to gladden your
eyes
Before it again starts to sink

You know you need to keep walking
Your tortured feet have gone numb
You can sense him stalking and hear the crows
squawking
And find you're half praying he come

You rest at last in a drift
And don his icy shawl
You cease to resist, it's time to enlist
And be forever held in his thrall

The Push Back

It is strange to find out
When someone's pushed and they've teased
Pulled at your struts 'til you're left on your knees
That they say it's you
You who were cruel and uncaring
You who's caused all of their despairing
As though the toxic
The controlling, corseting
Don't take too kindly to your boundary setting

Reflect and Renew

The year is finally waning
It is now at an end
I find myself reflecting
On the time we've had to spend

Time to look at what I've done
Put down that rosie glass
Acknowledge the good and bad
And times I was an ass

Put good memories in one pile
Keep them in good supply
To brighten a future day
And count your blessing by

The worse ones can be painful
But do not shy away
For those can give you learning
And growth, or so they say

But really when you come to
Look back at Auld Lang Syne
Mistakes will be minimised
So don't over malign

If you had to say goodbye
And sorrow's grip's securing
Recall that grief of any kind
Is your love enduring

Blessings counted, one by one
Time now to look ahead
Resolutions to be made
And broken down by Feb

But if you'll take my advice
Look at this last past year
See what gave you greatest joy
And keep holding that near

I raise a glass this Hogmanay
And send you best wishes
For your health and peace of mind
And much deserved blisses

The year is finally waning
It is now at an end
I look forward sanguinely
At what's around the bend